# Ben Lives
## That Irrepressible Dog is Back!

Skyhorse Publishing

Skyhorse Publishing books may be purchased in bulk at special discounts for sales promotion, corporate gifts, fund-raising, or educational purposes. Special editions can also be created to specifications. For details, contact the Special Sales Department, Skyhorse Publishing, 307 West 36th Street, 11th Floor, New York, NY 10018 or info@skyhorsepublishing.com.

Skyhorse® and Skyhorse Publishing® are registered trademarks of Skyhorse Publishing, Inc.®, a Delaware corporation.

www.skyhorsepublishing.com

10 9 8 7 6 5 4 3 2 1

Library of Congress Cataloging-in-Publication Data is available on file.

ISBN: 978-1-61608-397-7

Printed in China

*To Doris,*
*my wife, my life*

# FOREWORD

Fishing for muskies, Ben has whacked his master with the stick used to quiet big fish should they thrash wildly about the boat. "No, no, you idiot! The muskie, hit the muskie!" his owner implores him. Yes, Ben is back in full color, the happy-go-funny retriever strikes again. For instance, Ben stands so weighted down with new fishing gear he can hardly move. His boss observes, "Ben is now 'the complete angler'—unfortunately, he can't move." And hunting for ducks, his boss has missed another duck and says lamely, "Whoops, another miss, but who's counting?" Well, Ben is! Sitting in the back of the boat, he's keeping score on a pad. And Ben, sitting happily on a rocking chair, is being scolded by his boss, "What do you mean retired? You're only four years old!" Actually, Ben is nine years old, but he doesn't want to hear that.

Down through the ages dogs and their trusty and loyal companion—man—have served each other well. Man, by drafting dog and placing him in the front lines to get shot at, and using him for police and drug work to get shot at, and let's not forget hunting season, where he gets shot at. But this is about Ben, probably the sweetest, most intelligent retriever (with the exception, of course, of your dog). Although he looks like a large beagle, he is in truth a golden, a chihuahua, a poodle, and, of course, whatever else could jump the fence.

He's the only dog that can dress properly, knows how to fish, and when asked to do yard work, passes it on to his boss. He would like to apologize to the makers of dry dog food (which he makes fun of) and prefers to tip them off to a guy that will sell them some cans and juice cheap to keep the dry food wet. There's more to hunting than filling game bags, and Ben proves that every time they go hunting. Ben is our mixed breed sometime golden retriever who's been fetching us laughs for more than twenty years now, and he's at it again.

He's been thrown out of more dog shows than Lassie has entered. Ben isn't a purebred—it's obvious—but he has mastered the art of communication, which keeps him one step ahead of his master. Many hunters swear that their dog understands dozens of words, but just doesn't let on, fearing he'd be made to do chores around the house, guard the house when the family's away or, God forbid, go tracking in two feet of snow or retrieve ducks with a two foot chop on the bay. A simple "You talking to me?" serves the purpose of having people keep their distance. We have a lot to learn from Ben, most importantly that silence is golden, so pick up a *Ben Lives* for you or a friend. But let your dog know it and see it, too.

Let's join Ben and his boss as they find new adventures in familiar places, places you've seen and been to, and share them with old friends. Recently, I and my fishing buddy walked down to our favorite trout stream, and he paused as if to catch his breath and said, "It's getting tougher to wade. Even Ben is slowing down." I thought for a moment. "But we have our memories." "Yes," was his reply, "we have our memories."

See how many warm memories these cartoons bring back, and how much you loved those days.

—JOHN TROY
MAY 2011

"Maybe I'll just go fishing."

"If you're not going with me, Ben, nobody else is!"

"Getting ready for the crowd on opening day, Ben?"

"Nice costume, Ben, but you better rethink the candle bit."

"The barbecue is ready, but I don't know where Ben is."

"That's Ben's favorite scent line—it goes right to the picnic area."

"Open your lunch box, that'll wake him up."

"No, you don't need a *new* coop, you need a *clean* coop!"

"Ben, stop playing with your food!!"

"Ben, you didn't see our barbecue, did you?"

"Ben's been nailing poachers lately. These are his souvenirs."

"What do you mean you need a vacation? Your whole life is a vacation!"

"Don't worry, Ben, I'll have you loose before bow season starts."

"Nice tree stand, Ben. Where are you going to put the swimming pool?"

"What do you mean retired? You're only four years old!"

"Don't ask."

"*That's* your idea of feeding the fish?"

"Lighten up, Ben, your fish isn't going anywhere."

"We'll be late for dinner, dear. Ben tied himself to his vise."

"Ben, it's only February! Trout season is in APRIL!"

"That's nice of you to feed the goldfish, Ben."

"Now how did I guess you want to go walleye fishing? Hmm…"

"Ben jumped a black bear. Help me pry him loose."

"You wouldn't believe how windy it is outside!"

"All right, all right, I'll take you bass fishing!"

"Ben can't go hunting. He's still working on last summer's backlash."

"You don't practice ice fishing, you just go out and do it!"

"Oh well, I guess Ben doesn't want to go hunting. Too bad…"

"Ben chased a rabbit through a marijuana patch."

"Ben's idea of baiting a bear is to point at me."

"Ben's been tying flies for about a year now—matter of fact, it's the same fly."

"Guess what? Ben just tied a size 28 Royal Coachman!"

"'Just send me one of each' is no way to order from a catalog, Ben!"

"Plan on catching a lot of trophy fish this year, Ben?"

"Ben is now 'the complete angler.' Unfortunately, he can't move."

"Ben, I think you have the wrong idea about a whale watch."

"Y'know Ben, I've been thinking, we've been together a long time and we're due for a vacation—you to the Bahamas, me to anywhere but."

"Hang on, Ben, this road gets a little bumpy from here on in."

"I said throw me a *rope*, not a *rock*!"

"Ben, you're right, your old mittens make great puppy sleeping bags."

"I see you're all packed for a long camping trip."

"Ben doesn't believe in posting the old fashion way."

"No, Ben doesn't bite. It's to cut down on his binging."

"I said, ICE FISHING SEASON IS OVER!"

"No, Ben, that doesn't qualify as a one-hundred-foot cast. It's more like a one-hundred-foot *dangle.*"

"Don't rub it in, Ben!"

"Next time let *me* launch the boat."

"So let's see what you did to keep your favorite spot to yourself."

"I'll beat you to the top, Ben...hey, that's cheating!"

"That's still not quite right, Ben."

"Ben has a hard time letting go of bass fishing when hunting season starts."

"I don't get it. No bites, but something keeps taking my bait!"

"Guess who isn't allowed to use my new fishing rods?"

"Sometimes I feel that I'm spoiling you."

"Ben just realized that the worm he was putting on his hook is a real one."

"Ben's learning about catch and release."

"Ben, let's wait for a less windy day to practice our fly casting, okay?"

"Never mind barbless hooks, you need *hookless flies!*"

"Your fly casting lesson is over for the day, Ben. We've run out of Band-Aids and barbless hooks."

"No, no, I said it's a *nice fishing day*, not an *ice fishing day*."

"NO BEN, if they don't hit, change your fly! Don't dig worms!"

"I don't think that will fool anybody, Ben."

"It'll be a happy day in my life when you learn to cast horizontally."

"I think I've spotted the leak, Ben."

"Let's see who catches the biggest salmon, Ben, and no cheating—you have to use a fly rod."

"Nice to see you get a charge out of fly fishing, Ben."

"Talk nice to him, Ben, and maybe he'll quiet down."

"I've got a better idea, Ben. Call 911!"

"Ben isn't the best wader on the stream...whoops, here he comes now."

"Ben's a strong believer in 'back to basics.'"

"BEN!"

"Ben doesn't like to share his fishing spots."

"No, Ben, a noodling rod is not for bonking worm fishermen on the noodle."

"Ben is the main reason we switched to barbless hooks."

"Here comes Ben, job hunting again."

"Guy got your spot, Ben?"

"Ben likes to get in on the frenzy feeding."

"Ben is into fly fishing and trying to kick the worm habit 'cold turkey.'"

"Ben didn't know if he should go fly fishing or fly a kite, so here we are."

"Windy days like this, you really appreciate a good retriever."

"I don't mind keeping you warm, just watch your backcast!"

"What do you mean, 'They're rising to my bologna sandwich?'"

"With your new waders, Ben, you'll be able to fish deeper waters."

"Ben! That's not fly fishing!"

"So that's where the fish are—in shallow water!"

"No thank you, I can *see the fish!*"

"Getting a little territorial, aren't we, Ben?"

"That was a nice cast you had going for a minute, Ben."

"What fly are you using, Ben?"

"Nice hatch, something should start feeding pretty soon."

"That your dog trying to spawn again?"

"Boy, I could fish all day in this kind of weather! How about you, Ben?"

"When the wind is from the west, the fish will bite the best, eh Ben?"

"I get the feeling you've overpowered our bass boat, Ben."

"Since watching *Kung Fu*, Ben has a whole new way of fishing."

"When it comes to fish not hitting, Ben has zero tolerance."

"Nice to get away from Ben for a few hours, isn't it?"

"Ben is into 'catch and release,' trouble is it's always MY FISH he releases!"

"Ben's got a backlash you have to see to believe!"

"Centrifugal anti-backlash systems, friction cast selectors, magnetic spool control…
all the same to Ben."

"Ben doesn't leave the dock unless we have twenty-five pounds of ice in the live well."

"Ben, your backlashes wind up in the darndest places."

"C'mon, Ben, lighten up and troll the right way."

"Okay, okay, it makes a nice tie pin. Now get it off me!"

"Ben, I don't think 'catch and release' applies to our live bass!"

"You oughta see the size of the crawdads I got for bait."

"What do you mean you have the best looking lure ever made?"

"No, it's *not* undersized, and no you're *not* throwing it back!"

"I think dogs should have *fishing* licenses, too!"

"No, Ben, that's NOT catch and release!"

"Can't you practice catch and release on your end of the boat?!"

"Just throw him back, Ben, and forget the lecture."

"Sure you don't need a net, Ben?"

"I'll have this muskie in the boat in a minute, Ben!"

"No, no, the fish scent goes on the bait, not me!!"

"So we didn't catch any fish, Ben—who cares? We were able to spend quality time together on a splendid day, enjoying not only the great outdoors, but also each other's company. Not only that…"

"*Now* do you know why I don't let you gaff?!"

"Make sure we're in the boat before you start the motor, okay, Ben?"

"Next time we take MY boat."

"Ben, slow down so I can net the fish!"

"You found a way to save us on gas money? This I've got to see."

"Will you cut out the dramatics? It's plastic!!"

"Ben, your eating habits are getting out of control."

"Stop making fun of the fish I catch!"

"I never saw anybody that liked ice fishing so much."

"Kind of rushing the deer season, aren't you Ben?

"Boy, when you go back to basics, you don't fool around!"

"Time to get your priorities straight, Ben!"

"Next time bring a camera!"

"Bad news for anyone in Ben's fishing spot."

"Relax, Ben, I don't think anybody'll be in our spot today."

"How long do you intend to make fun of my 8-horsepower motor?"

"Slow down, Ben, we're running out of equipment!"

"How come I don't hear you complaining about the heat?"

"NOW ARE YOU SATISFIED!?"

"Hey back there! We're on vacation!!"

"Don't even think about it!"

"Ben has this silly idea about hunting geese with a hang glider. He's home working on it now…"

"Give it a yank, it might just fly out."

"Give you a real gun? Are you kidding?"

"Don't shoot, I think it's BEN!"

"It's going to be a while before I take you hunting again!"

"Can't say this high grass really bothers Ben."

"How about pointing them while they're still on the ground!"

"Yessir, Ben, you must've run that rabbit for twenty miles…too bad it was in a straight line."

"Candy wrapper. Nice point, though."

"That's Ben's idea of affirmative action."

"Ben is really catching on to retrieving. All we have to do now is get him to do it in our direction."

"Training school, here we come again!"

"What do you mean, 'The old eyes start to go when you hit the big 6-0!' I'm only thirty-two!"

"Those old tom turkeys can be pretty tough, Ben, but stick with me and you'll be all right."

"Here they come, Ben, let's sit down real quick so we don't scare them off!"

"You'll get there first all right."

"Here they come, Ben, get ready with your duck call!"

"No, Ben, we don't flip a coin to see who gets it!"

"Darn, missed again! Sorry, Ben, I know how eager you are to make a retrieve."

"You're not really big on duck hunting, are you?"

"This is your idea of a 'catch and release' duck hunt?"

"I think you'd find it easier if you used two of them."

"So what if you can't hold a gun with those mittens on! You don't have a hunting license anyway!"

"Tracking game in snow sure is fun, Ben. Trouble is the only tracks are ours!"

"I said HUNTING, not HAUNTING!"

"I don't know what he's doing, and it's not in the field manual, either."

"If you're going to be my hunting dog, you'll have to do better than that!"

"Don't get unsnagged, Ben, DON'T GET UNSNAGGED!"

"Ben's motto is 'Take a puppy fishing today.'"

"You give a whole new meaning, Ben, to the word 'backcast.'"

"That's your idea for chumming for bass?!"

"Your bass must weigh ten pounds, Ben. Whoa, what's this? My sinkers, my pliers, watch, knife…"

"We're a half mile from shore, so whose hat do you think it is?!"

"When they don't hit on flies, *they don't hit on flies. That's it, Ben!*"

"Cool it with the long fish stories, Ben, Christmas Eve is busy for Santa!"

"Yessiree, Ben, they don't make decoys like they used to. Matter of fact, they never did."

"This is a survival test, Ben, not a picnic!"

"It's okay, Ben, he left your gifts under the tree!"

"Now that's what I call a real ATV!"

QUIZ: Can you name the kind of trout Ben is imitating?

"So that's why our electric bill has been so high!!"

"Raindrops keep falling on my head, but that doesn't mean…."